What Grows?

by Miriam Sklar

ISBN: 978-1-338-75087-4
Illustrated by John Lund

Published by Scholastic Inc., 557 Broadway, New York, NY 10012

10 9 8 7 6 5 4   68   25 26 27/0

Printed in Jiaxing, China. First printing, January 2021.

A seed grows.

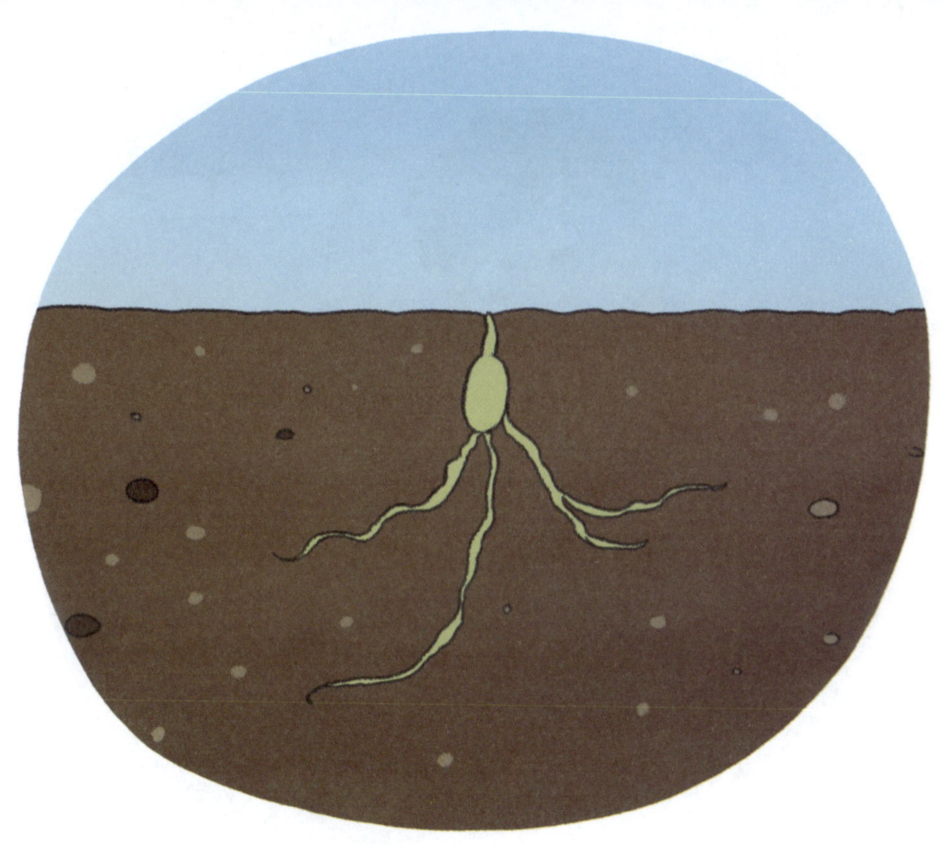

A root grows.

A stem grows.

A vine grows.

A flower grows.

A pumpkin grows.

A kid grows!